Happy Chinese New Year.

Children Activity Books with 30 Coloring Pages of Chinese Dragons, Red Lanterns, Fireworks, Firecrackers, and Many Festive Celebrating Objects for Boys and Girls Age 3-8 to Celebrate Their Fun Chinese New Year!

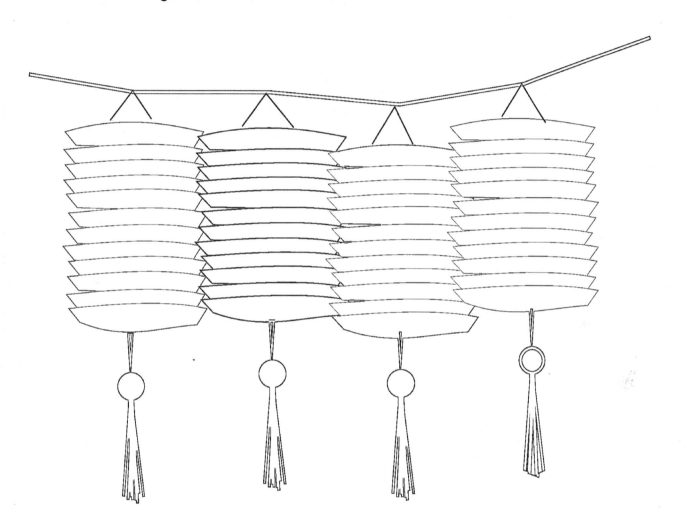

Copyright © 2015 by Happy Chinese Children Coloring Books

All right reserved. This book or any portion thereof may not be reproduced or used in any manner whatsoever without the express written permission of the publisher, except for the use of brief quotations in a book review.

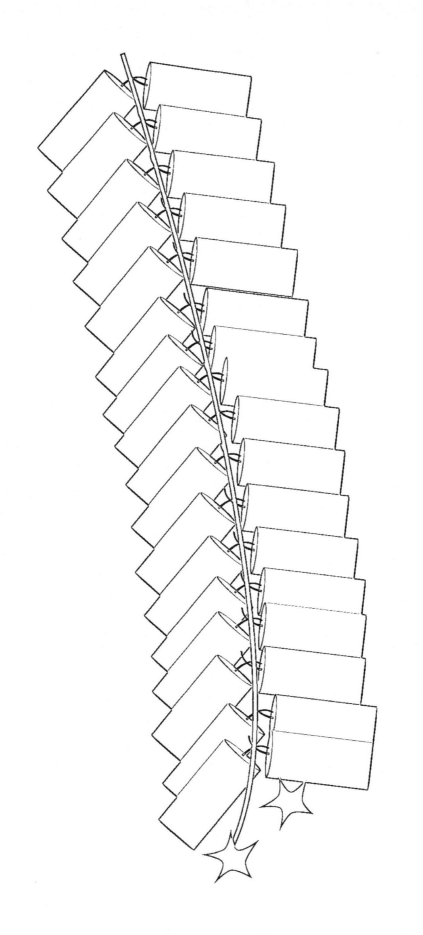

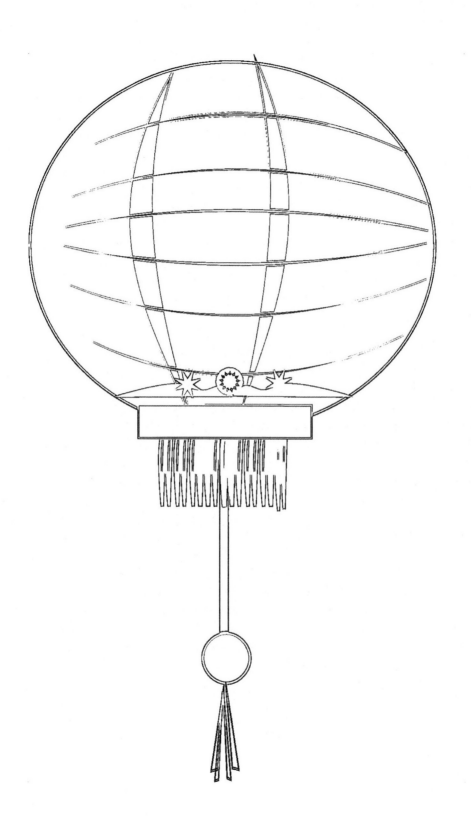